# CONTENTS

4

# EARTH

**Elisa Peters**

**PowerKiDS**
press.

New York

Published in 2013 by The Rosen Publishing Group, Inc.
29 East 21st Street, New York, NY 10010

First Edition

Editor: Amelie von Zumbusch
Book Design: Kate Laczynski

Photo Credits: Cover Stocktrek/Digital Vision/Getty Images; p. 4 Jupiterimages/Creatas/Thinkstock; pp. 6, 8, 10, 12, 16, 24 (rock) Shutterstock.com; pp. 14, 24 (moon) Comstock/Comstock/Thinkstock; pp. 18, 24 (sun) Jupiterimages/Photos.com/Thinkstock; p. 20 Ablestock.com/Ablestock.com/Thinkstock; p. 22 iStockphoto/Thinkstock.

Library of Congress Cataloging-in-Publication Data

Peters, Elisa.
  Earth / By Elisa Peters. — 1st ed.
    p. cm. — (Powerkids readers: the universe)
  Includes index.
  ISBN 978-1-4488-7387-6 (library binding) — ISBN 978-1-4488-7467-5 (pbk.) —
ISBN 978-1-4488-7539-9 (6-pack)
  1. Earth–Juvenile literature. I. Title.
  QB631.4.P46 2013
  525—dc23

                              2011048265

Manufactured in the United States of America

CPSIA Compliance Information: Batch #CS12PK: For Further Information contact Rosen Publishing, New York, New York at 1-800-237-9932

We live on Earth.

It is the third planet from the Sun.

8

The Nile is its longest river.

Earth is made of **rock**.

12

Water covers most of Earth.

14

The **Moon** causes tides.

Earth circles the **Sun**.

18

A full circle takes one year.

20

Earth spins as it circles.

It is our home!

# WORDS TO KNOW

Moon

rocks

Sun

# WEBSITES

Due to the changing nature of Internet links, PowerKids Press has developed an online list of websites related to the subject of this book. This site is updated regularly. Please use this link to access the list:
www.powerkidslinks.com/pkrtu/earth/